Published by Hallmark Books,
a division of Hallmark Cards, Inc.,
Kansas City, MO 64141
Visit us on the Web at www.Hallmark.com.

Editorial Director: Todd Hafer
Editor: Theresa Trinder
Art Director: Kevin Swanson
Designer: Alison T. Bauer
Illustrator: Peg Carlson-Hoffman
Lettering Artist: Jim Fedor
Production Artist: Dan C. Horton

10 9 8 7 6 5 4 3 2 1

ISBN 978-1-59530-168-0

BOK5522

Printed and bound in China

Note-Worthy

a guide to writing great personal notes

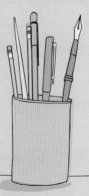

BY ANGELA ENSMINGER & KEELY CHACE

Table of Contents

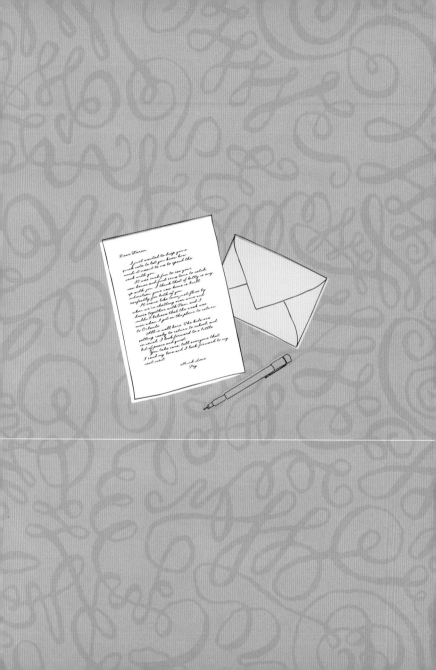

Authors' Note

Dear Reader,

    This book is all about helping you put your feelings into words. Written words. It's that simple. And while it offers plenty of practical information on note writing for life's most common occasions—including the six steps to writing a great note every time—this isn't a book about etiquette, rules of grammar, or the "art" of note writing. That's just not us.

    This is a book about the "heart" of note writing. It's about why you write in the first place—and what makes a note memorable, impactful, and personal. It's about how great it feels to know that your words are going to matter to someone. This is a book that will help you to build the confidence—and the skills—to never again sit in front of a blank piece of paper and wonder "What should I say?"

    Sound good? Then this book is for you. Plus, we think you'll really like it. And use it. And that makes us feel good.

    So go ahead, dig in! Bookmark and dog-ear the pages. Underline sentences. Circle things you want to remember. Write in the margins! As long as you start (and keep on) writing great notes, we won't mind one bit. Promise.

    Here's to writing great notes. Here's to you!

    Sincerely,

Angela Ensminger & Keely Chace

Introduction

Let's face it—lately, we're busier than ever. Our days are jam-packed. Our calendars are booked solid. Our to-do lists are downright intimidating. With so much to do and so little time to do it, why would any of us even consider sitting down with a pen and paper when it would be so much easier to e-mail, call, or text message?

In an increasingly complicated world, the answer is refreshingly simple: Because personal notes tell people that they are worth our time. That they matter to us. That we care.

And while personal notes could never completely replace our faster, easier methods of communication, there are times the power of a personal note can really make a difference.

Personal notes can brighten up regular days and help celebrate special ones. They can help ease heartache or rekindle romance. They can help us reach out—whether across the street or across an ocean—and remind the people in our lives that we are thinking of them, that we appreciate them, and—most of all—that they are worth the time and effort it took to tell them so. And in a world where time can be measured by the nanosecond, that message can mean a lot.

using this book

Becoming a great note writer is not as difficult as it sounds.

In fact, learning to write notes is a lot like learning to cook a new dish. At first, you'll probably follow the recipe word for word. Eventually, after you make the dish several times, you'll allow your instincts and experience to take over. You might add a favorite spice or substitute some ingredients for others. And after a while, you probably won't even have to look at the recipe anymore . . . making that dish will just come naturally.

That's how it is with writing great notes, too. Once you get the hang of the basic steps, your own intuition and creativity kick in.

Right off the bat, this book will teach you our basic six-step "recipe" for writing great personal notes. It will be the foundation of every personal note you write. Understand the six simple steps, and the rest is simple!

Speaking of simple . . . this book is easy to find your way around. In fact, we've organized it into three main chapters—each focused on one of life's most common note-writing occasions: Gratitude, Support & Sympathy, and Celebration.

Each chapter reminds you of the basic six-step note-writing recipe, then provides ideas and inspiration, useful words and phrases, and numerous sample notes to draw from. The fourth and final chapter offers some special "above-and-beyond" information on things like what paper to use and how to address an envelope.

Remember—writing great personal notes is easy. Just give it a try. They're all made from the same six ingredients. But how they turn out in the end—spicy, rich, sweet, or fluffy—is completely up to you.

the 6 steps

A great note consists of six simple steps, so writing one is as easy as 1-2-3 (well, 1-2-3-4-5-6).

Dear Anne, —①

Thank you so much for the beautiful vase ② *you gave me for my birthday. What a thoughtful gift—and it makes such a* ③ *wonderful addition to my kitchen! In fact, it's filled with sunflowers right now. I'm so glad, too, that you could join* ④ *us for dinner*—*an evening of talking and laughing with my very best friends was the best birthday gift I could have received! Thank you again for your thoughtful birthday gift* ⑤ *and for your year-round friendship.*

Sincerely, —⑥
Elaine

① GREET THE RECIPIENT
② CLEARLY STATE WHY YOU ARE WRITING
③ ELABORATE ON WHY YOU ARE WRITING
④ BUILD THE RELATIONSHIP
⑤ RESTATE WHY YOU ARE WRITING
⑥ GIVE YOUR REGARDS

① GREET THE RECIPIENT

This step, known as the salutation, or greeting, is your note's opening number. In just one line, it tells the recipient this note is written just for him or her. It also sets the tone for the rest of your message. These first few words can make a strong first impression—and you want that first impression to be as good as possible. Here are some tips for starting your note out right.

choose your words wisely

Be sure to maintain the right level of formality in your notes. If you're not sure, ask yourself this question: How would you greet this person if you ran into him or her in a restaurant? If you would feel even a little bit uncomfortable saying *Lou* or *Betty* in person, then you shouldn't do so in writing. Use his or her last name with the correct title (*Mr., Mrs., Ms., Dr., Professor,* etc.). When in doubt, err on the side of formality.

first words

Dear is the most common and universally appropriate salutation. It works for every kind of note—from formal to casual, business to pleasure. You can use this salutation for the vast majority of the notes you write.

For those "exception-to-the-rule" notes where a more creative salutation is appropriate, consider:

- more casual openers like *Hi, Becky*; *Hello, Tony!*; or simply *Amanda!*
- holiday greetings such as *Happy Father's Day, Dad*; *To my Valentine*; or *Merry Christmas, Meghan!*
- occasion-appropriate phrases like *Congratulations, Linda!*; *To the soon-to-be mom*; or *Happy Birthday, Mrs. Bauer!*

check and double-check

Unless you are 200% sure, always double-check that you're using the correct spelling of the recipient's name, as well as the names of anyone else mentioned in your note. Spelling someone's name incorrectly sends the message that you did not take the time—or give her the attention—she deserves.

the name game

Nicknames can be tricky. Not sure if Rodney would like to see *Rod* or *The Rodster* in writing? Use your best judgment—and, more often than not, his full first name.

For close relationships, like significant others, family, or very close friends, consider using a special name or term of endearment . . . but only if you're sure he'll like it.

Think about whether you might want to include another person in your greeting. (Did a gift come from two people? Does your cousin have a small child at home who would love to be included?) It's absolutely okay to add as many recipients as you see fit!

examples

- *Dear Jackson,*
- *Dear Melinda and Jerry,*
- *Dear Dr. McMurphy,*
- *Hi, Lisa!*
- *Dear Mrs. Garcia, José, Ana, and Ramón,*
- *Dear Shannon,*
- *Alexis,*
- *Congratulations, Lindsay!*
- *Merry Christmas, Mom and Dad!*
- *Hi Honey,*

② CLEARLY STATE WHY YOU ARE WRITING

This is the first sentence in the body of your note— your chance to come right out and let the recipient know why you're writing. This should be a simple and straight- forward first line that captures the recipient's attention immediately. It's this first line that sets up the coming message so that it really makes an impact.

be clear and concise

Clearly state your reason for writing. You'll have plenty of opportunity to elaborate in coming lines, so limit your adjectives and descriptive words to keep this line as simple as possible.

If it's a thank-you note, the words *thank you* should be front and center.

For sympathy notes, express your sympathy in a direct, straightforward way. Your message may get a little garbled if you try to sound poetic or overly formal. Just be yourself. The recipient will appreciate it and your note's main message (that you care) will come through loud and clear.

know your audience

The language, tone, and details of a personal note can vary depending on who you are writing to. For formal, business, and sympathy notes, stick with clear, simple language. For more casual notes—or notes to people with whom you share a close relationship—don't be afraid to have some fun. But when in doubt, keep it warm and straightforward.

Say you received a blue sweater for your birthday. Depending on who gave it to you, your note's first line can vary.

If it's from your colleague, acquaintance, or someone you have a formal relationship with, try:

Thank you so much for the beautiful blue sweater you gave me for my birthday.

This note's first line uses a strong yet general adjective (*beautiful*) and is sure to mention details of the gift (the color), as well as why it was given (as a birthday gift).

If it's from your mom, sister, friend, or other person you feel close to, try:

Thanks so much for the fantastic sweater!

This note uses more upbeat language (*fantastic*). It doesn't require the same level of detail (the color or the reason for giving). There is an understanding between the sender and recipient that it's clear what sweater the writer's talking about.

> Remember—you'll have the opportunity
> to elaborate in coming lines,
> so keep the first one short and sweet!

examples
- *Thank you so much for helping us move last weekend.*
- *John and I want to thank you both for hosting such a fantastic dinner party on Friday!*

- *Thank you very much for the generous gift certificate.*
- *Just a note to let you know how much I enjoyed our date on Saturday.*
- *Please accept my heartfelt sympathy on the loss of your husband and father.*
- *You have been in my thoughts lately.*
- *Congratulations on your promotion!*
- *I was so excited to hear you are expecting twins!*
- *I wanted to be the first to wish you a very happy holiday!*
- *Happy Valentine's Day, Valentine!*

③ ELABORATE ON WHY YOU ARE WRITING

This is your chance to elaborate—in one to two sentences—on why you're sending your note. It's also the place where your personality can really come through! After all, great notes distinguish themselves from so-so notes by the details and examples they use to bring their words to life.

Here are some examples of how you can do just that.

show you know him (or her)

- Compliment him. Talk about his good taste in gifts, his skill in the kitchen (or making reservations!), the talents that got him where he is today, the strength he is showing in the face of difficulty, or the memorable and admirable aspects of his personality.

- Pay attention. What's going on in his life? Does he have a favorite hobby or pastime? Has something significant just happened (or about to happen) in his life? Ask about it.
- Get specific. Add meaningful details where you can. Mention something he's done in the past, something you've noticed about him (a toast he gave, a suit he wore). This shows that you are observant and remember details—that he made an impression on you and he matters to you.
- Share memories. Whether they're from last week or twenty years ago, shared memories are one of the best ways to keep up (or even rekindle) a relationship. For thank-you and celebratory notes, look back to a great time shared or a particular situation that comes to mind. For sympathynotes, write about what made the deceased special and memorable to you. Share a good memory or funny story the recipient might enjoy. If you didn't know the deceased, consider acknowledging his or her importance to the recipient. Focus on the person, not their death.

share your feelings

As you write, elaborate on how you are feeling about the event, occasion, or situation at hand. Sharing your honest feelings is the sincerest form of emotional connecting you can do—and that authenticity will come through in your note.

- Write about how much better you felt after receiving help, a great gift, or sharing some time together.
- Think about the person as well as what's going on in her life—and don't skimp on warmth or affection.
- List several good wishes for a special day.
- For difficult situations, don't be afraid to tell someone your heart is going out to her or your thoughts are with her—it will help her know she's not alone.

details, details, details

This is the place to add the one-of-a-kind specifics that only you can.

- For a thank-you note for a gift, write about how you're using it or any plans you have for it.
- For a thank-you note after a dinner, event, or overnight stay, call out something specific you enjoyed or something that stands out in your mind.
- To express thanks for help or support, tell the recipient how much he helped you out and how much better you're feeling now.

just heard some news?

This is the place where you can discuss your feelings about the news that might have prompted your note—

from good news (like a promotion, new baby, or an engagement) to sad news (such as an illness, accident, or death).

- Talk about why it's such good news, sad news, or surprising news.
- Let her know how and when you heard the news, if not from her, and be sure to describe your reaction.
- Remember—it's important to verify news you hear "through the grapevine" before sending a note. Avoiding embarrassment is always a good thing.

examples

- *Your help—from packing boxes to driving the van—made the whole move so much smoother. I can't imagine how long it would have taken without you!*
- *The meal was exceptional, the wine was delicious, and the company was the best! We cannot remember a time when we laughed so hard.*
- *It was such a nice surprise to find it in our mailbox. We're touched that you remembered our favorite take-out restaurant!*
- *The picnic lunch you made was really good (and really fun). Those were the best chocolate chip cookies I've ever had. And I'm still reeling about flying that kite! It made me feel like a kid again!*

- *He was such a kind and wonderful man. I don't think there was a single person who didn't enjoy his cheerful company.*
- *I know that your treatments have been difficult, but I want to remind you how many people are thinking of you, pulling for you, and sending lots of love your way!*
- *I was so thrilled to hear from Lucy that you'll be managing the entire Waterson account. It's a tremendous job, but there isn't a single person who is better suited for it than you.*
- *I can only imagine how thrilled you and Dan are. I know how much starting a family has meant to both of you. And just look—your dream is coming true!*
- *Okay, okay, I know—Dad's probably been scouring the local tree farms for weeks now, and Mom's probably turned the den into gift-wrap central. But at our house, Christmas is just kicking in, and I want you to know how much we're thinking of you.*
- *I'm so excited to be spending our eighth happy-heart day together. Time sure flies when you're having fun!*

④ BUILD THE RELATIONSHIP

Think of this part of the note as where you'll "compliment and look ahead." It's about appreciating where you are now in your relationship and looking ahead to the future. This important step, which is often just one or two short sentences, can really drive home the message that you really care about who you're sending it to—today and tomorrow!

come right out and say it

Because the preceding step uses specific details, stories, and feelings, it usually contains a lot of information for the recipient to process. Therefore, it's important that this step be more direct, to the point, and easy to understand.

compliment

A great personal note makes the recipient feel good about herself and your relationship.

- If you're comfortable with this idea, compliment her on her thoughtfulness, kindness, or creativity (whatever applies!) and remind her that she holds a special place in your life.
- Use this step as your chance to say some things you might forget to say on a daily—or even monthly—basis.
- Mention the importance of (and your gratitude for) your relationship.
- For special days, like birthdays, holidays, or the anniversary of a special event, talk about the meaning of the day and what it means in your relationship.

look ahead

- Look forward to an upcoming event (large or small) or, simply, the next time you'll see the recipient.
- Let him know he matters to you and you'd like to talk or get together soon.
- Recall a time he helped you and offer to return the favor.
- Offer help or advice if appropriate.
- Not a close relationship? Just tell him you will be thinking about him and wishing him well.
- Express confidence in his future success.
- For notes of support, sympathy, or even congratulations, let the recipient know you will continue to keep him in your thoughts. Reaffirm the relationship by looking forward to spending time or talking with him.

examples

- *You're such a good friend to spend your Saturday sweating with us, and we truly appreciate it. The next time you need help, you know who to call!*
- *You are incredible hosts, and even more—you're great friends. I'm already looking forward to the next time we can get together.*
- *You are so sweet to think of us—and you chose the perfect gift to help make life easier while we're both*

working so much overtime. Maybe you'll drop by and share dinner with us next weekend?

- *I know we've only been dating a short time, but I want you to know how much you mean to me. In fact, I feel like the luckiest guy in the world.*
- *Please take good care of yourselves and each other during this difficult time, and know how many thoughts and prayers are with you all.*
- *Your strength, humor, and amazing attitude are stronger than all of this. I can't wait to come visit you on Thursday.*
- *Your creativity, passion, and talent are downright inspiring! I can't wait to come by your new office next time I'm downtown.*
- *Those little babies have no idea what great parents they're going to have! I can't wait to see you guys at Lynn's house next weekend.*
- *In fact, everyone is counting the days until you arrive. Madison has even started getting her room ready for her Nana and Gramps. Needless to say, we're all so excited to see you!*
- *You treat me like your Valentine all year long . . . so today it's my turn. We've got special dinner plans, so be home by 5:30 sharp!*

⑤ RESTATE WHY YOU ARE WRITING

Great personal notes come full circle—by ending the way they began. In one short sentence, this simple but very important step reiterates why you wrote and reinforces your note's main message.

keep it short . . . but sweet

Save the really good stuff for the body of your note—and make this step simple and straightforward.

- Express your gratitude, support, or excitement again.
- Restate wishes and thoughts.
- Offer sympathy at the close of the note.
- Let the reader know you'll be missing her, thinking about her, or praying for her.
- Use holiday greetings when appropriate (*Have a happy New Year!*).
- When appropriate, those three little words (*I love you*) are a great bet.

examples

- *Again, Jackson, thank you so much!*
- *Thanks again for a truly enjoyable time.*
- *Thank you so much.*
- *So thanks again for another fantastic weekend— I can't wait to see you on Friday!*
- *My heart goes out to you.*

- *Until then, know I'm thinking of you.*
- *Again, my heartfelt congratulations on this well-deserved promotion.*
- *Enjoy this wonderful time—I'm so thrilled for you both!*
- *So, until the 22nd, we're sending holiday wishes—from our house to yours!*
- *And until then, Happy Valentine's Day! I love you.*

⑥ GIVE YOUR REGARDS

This is it—you're about to cross your note's finish line. Why not do it with style?

Personal notes vary in tone and content. There are formal notes for business and serious situations, fun notes for congratulations and festive occasions, warm-hearted notes of thanks, and so many more. And while *Sincerely* is a universally appropriate closing, good for almost every note you'll ever write, many notes can benefit from creative, unique, or personal parting words.

avoid redundancy

When choosing a regard, try to avoid repeating anything you've already written in the body of the note. For example, if your note begins *Please accept my deepest sympathy*, then *With deepest sympathy* isn't a great closing. *Sincerely* or *My condolences* are better choices.

when to keep it simple

Business notes, support or sympathy notes, or any note to someone with whom you do not share a close relationship are all well-ended with *Sincerely*. As with salutations, when in doubt, keep your regards simple and straightforward.

conventions for regards

The general rule is to capitalize only the first word of your regards. Subsequent words should start with a lowercase letter unless they would normally be capitalized. Follow your regards with a comma.

• *Sincerely,*	• *Best wishes,*
Anthony	*Chandra*

defying convention

If the relationship is close or the note is casual, feel free to use a regard of your own invention . . . or to skip the regard altogether and just sign your name. It's your note, after all.

examples

• *Your friends,*	• *Sincerely,*
Lisa and George	*Your neighbors, the Johnsons*
• *Sincerely,*	• *Yours,*
Christine and John	*Alan*

· *Sincerely,*
  Alice Moore
· *Love,*
  Carlena
· *Sincerely,*
  Ellen Harrison

· *Love you,*
  Pamela
· *Lots of love,*
  Melanie, Dave, Madison, and Luke
· *XOXO,*
  Your loving (and lucky!) wife

some more great endings

Drawing a blank? Running out of steam? Here are a few ideas for great endings.

FAMILY AND CLOSE FRIENDS

Fondly, Warmly, Yours truly, Lovingly, Love, Lots of love, My/Our love, With love, Your (son), Your (friend), Your loving (mother), Your devoted (sister)

GRATITUDE

Gratefully, Gratefully yours, With thanks, With gratitude, With deepest gratitude, With love and gratitude, Your grateful (friend), My thanks, Many thanks

CONGRATULATIONS

My/Our sincere congratulations, My/Our heartfelt congratulations, With warmest congratulations, With admiration, With love and pride

ROMANTIC LOVE

Love, My love, All my love, My love forever, I love you, Yours, Yours always, Forever yours, Eternally yours,

Always, Tenderly, Passionately, Affectionately, XOXO, Your loving (wife)

COMFORT AND CHEER

Thinking of you, With warmest thoughts, With caring thoughts, With warmest wishes, With hope

CONDOLENCE

With sympathy, With deepest sympathy, In sympathy, My/Our condolences

RELIGIOUS

God bless, Blessings, Bless you, My/Our love and prayers, With hope and prayers

putting it all together

With each step in this chapter, you've been given examples of how that particular step might look and sound. So what happens when you put all six steps together? The answer is simple . . . you've got a great personal note!

On the following pages, we've combined the examples included on the previous pages. Now you can see for yourself how a great note comes together, step by easy step.

great example notes

Dear Jackson,

Thank you so much for helping us move last weekend. Your help—from packing boxes to driving the van—made the whole move so much smoother. I can't imagine how long it would have taken without you! You're such a good friend to spend your Saturday sweating with us, and we truly appreciate it. The next time you need help, you know who to call! Again, Jackson, thank you so much.

Your friends,
Lisa and George

THANK YOU

Dear Melinda and Jerry,

John and I want to thank you both for hosting such a fantastic dinner party on Friday! The meal was exceptional, the wine was delicious, and the company was the best! We cannot remember a time when we laughed so hard. You are incredible hosts, and even more—you're great friends. I'm already looking forward to the next time we can get together. Thanks again for a truly enjoyable time.

Sincerely,
Christine and John

THANK YOU

Dear Dr. McMurphy,

Thank you very much for the generous gift certificate. It was such a nice surprise to find it in our mailbox. We're touched that you remembered our favorite take-out restaurant. You are so sweet to think of us—and you chose the perfect gift to help make life easier while we're both working so much overtime. Maybe you'll drop by and share dinner with us next weekend? Thank you so much.

Sincerely,
Your Neighbors, the Johnsons

Hi, Lisa!

Just a note to let you know how much I enjoyed our date on Saturday. The picnic lunch you made was really good (and really fun). Those were the best chocolate chip cookies I've ever had. And I'm still reeling about flying that kite! It made me feel like a kid again! I know we've only been dating a short time, but I want you to know how much you mean to me. In fact, I feel like the luckiest guy in the world. So thanks again for another fantastic weekend—I can't wait to see you on Friday.

Yours,
Alan

Dear Mrs. Garcia, José, Ana, and Ramón,

Please accept my heartfelt sympathy on the loss of your husband and father. He was such a kind and wonderful man. I don't think there was a single person who didn't enjoy his cheerful company. Please take good care of yourselves and each other during this difficult time, and know how many thoughts and prayers are with you all. My heart goes out to you.

Sincerely,
Alice Moore

SYMPATHY

Dear Shannon,

You have been in my thoughts lately. I know that your treatments have been difficult, but I want to remind you how many people are thinking of you, pulling for you, and sending lots of love your way! Your strength, humor, and amazing attitude are stronger than all of this. I can't wait to come visit you on Thursday. Until then, know I'm thinking of you.

Love,
Carlena

SUPPORT

CONGRATULATIONS

Alexis,

Congratulations on your promotion! I was so thrilled to hear from Lucy that you'll be managing the entire Waterson account. It's a tremendous job, but there isn't a single person who is better suited for it than you. Your creativity, passion, and talent are downright inspiring! I can't wait to come by your new office next time I'm downtown. Again, my heartfelt congratulations on this well-deserved promotion.

Sincerely,
Ellen Harrison

CONGRATULATIONS

Congratulations, Lindsay!

I was so excited to hear you are expecting twins! I can only imagine how thrilled you and Dan are. I know how much starting a family has meant to both of you. And just look—your dream is coming true! Those little babies have no idea what great parents they're going to have! I can't wait to see you guys at Lynn's house next weekend. Enjoy this wonderful time—I'm so thrilled for you both!

Love you,
Pamela

Merry Christmas, Mom and Dad!

I wanted to be the first to wish you a very happy holiday! Okay, okay, I know—Dad's probably been scouring the local tree farms for weeks now, and Mom's probably turned the den into gift-wrap central. But at our house, Christmas is just kicking in, and I want you to know how much we're thinking of you. In fact, everyone is counting the days until you arrive. Madison has even started getting her room ready for her Nana and Gramps. Needless to say, we're all so excited to see you! So, until the 22nd, we're sending holiday wishes—from our house to yours!

Lots of love,
Melanie, Dave, Madison, and Luke

Hi, Honey,

Happy Valentine's Day, Valentine! I'm so excited to be spending our eighth happy-heart day together. Time sure flies when you're having fun! You treat me like your Valentine all year long . . . so today it's my turn. We've got special dinner plans, so be home by 5:30 sharp! And until then, Happy Valentine's Day! I love you.

XOXO,
Your loving (and lucky!) wife

Notes of Thanks

Thank-you notes are the single most common type of note we write. If only there were a class in school that taught us how to do it! Then we wouldn't feel so helpless when faced with that blank piece of paper and a task that seems too difficult for words.

Still, knowing how to put pen to paper and write a great thank-you note is a skill worth learning, no matter how old you are. It feels good to send one. It feels good to get one. And writing one doesn't have to feel like a homework assignment. A little guidance, practice, and good humor is all it takes.

why thank-you notes matter

Whether it's a simple homemade dinner, a generous check, or a heartfelt chat—when people do something nice for us, they're giving us the gifts of their thought and time. And a thank-you note acknowledges this. It does more than just thank someone for what he or she did. It's the best way (and sometimes the only way) to return someone's kindness. A great thank-you note says "I noticed what you did, I appreciate your kindness, I appreciate your time . . . I appreciate you."

reasons for sending

Some of the things we're most grateful for aren't things at all. Consider some of these expected (and not-so-expected) reasons to put pen to paper and say thanks!

some obvious occasions for thanks

- for wedding and bridal shower gifts
- for baby gifts
- for graduation gifts
- for gifts for religious rites of passage like baptism, communion, bar or bat mitzvah, etc.
- for housewarming, hostess, and hospitality gifts
- for hosting a dinner, event, or party in your honor
- for encouragement during an illness or recovery

· for expressions of sympathy, such as cards, flowers, or donations

some not-so-obvious occasions

· for gifts for birthdays and holidays (even though most holidays are annual events—you can still say thanks!)
· for gifts from someone's kitchen
· for house-sitting, pet-sitting, or babysitting
· for lending tools, equipment, or a vehicle
· for help with errands, moving, or transportation
· for sharing advice or experience
· for tutoring your child
· for help with a new baby
· for support during a divorce or breakup
· for encouragement or help on the job
· for dinner or a night on the town
· for throwing a great party
· for offering a place to stay

timing

Here's a good rule of thumb for thank-you notes: timeliness is thoughtfulness. Try to send your note within three days of an event or receipt of a gift, while it's still fresh in your mind—and the recipient's, too.

That said, late is better than never. If your note will arrive later than a week after an event or a gift's arrival, apologize for the delay, but don't dwell on it. People will understand.

For support or encouragement, it's good to try to send a thank-you as soon as possible, but because these notes are often occasioned by difficult times, the better-late-than-never rule applies more than ever. People will understand if it takes you a while to write a note, and they'll certainly appreciate it when it arrives.

> *for the bride and groom*
> For wedding gifts, etiquette says you have three months (rather than three days) to send your notes. But try not to wait much longer than that, no matter how long it takes you to address all those envelopes.

FAQs

BUT . . . WHAT IF IT WAS AWFUL?

Even if you didn't enjoy the gift, party, or the overnight stay, you can still thank someone for the time and effort they put into it. Clearly state your gratitude for the gesture, then try and pick out something you did like and focus on that. A thoughtful gesture? A unique item? A great dish? A comfy bed? Details like this will help you focus on the positive. Remember—even if a gift or experience wasn't your favorite, sending a personal thank-you note is still a nice thing to do.

I HAVEN'T WRITTEN MANY THANK-YOU NOTES IN THE PAST. WILL PEOPLE THINK I'M WEIRD IF I START SENDING THEM NOW?

You might think it'll surprise people who know you if you suddenly start writing thank-you notes. Though it might at first, ask yourself this: is this the kind of change your friends and family are likely to complain about? If you still feel funny, start out slow. Send a thank-you note the next time someone gives you a gift, treats you to dinner, or goes out of his or her way to help you. See how the recipient reacts. See what kind of difference it makes. The only question you might have is why you didn't start writing thank-you notes sooner! So be confident about turning over a new leaf (or a new note card).

DO I HAVE TO WRITE A THANK-YOU NOTE FOR EVERY NICE THING PEOPLE DO FOR ME? CAN'T I E-MAIL OR CALL TO SAY THANKS?

The quick answer: of course you can still e-mail or call. You never—and we repeat, never—have to write a thank-you note. We don't think the pen will ever replace any of our faster, more modern methods of communication. But most of us can agree that life presents us with occasions when the kind of message a person can hold in her hands is the only kind that will do—and there are plenty of other occasions when that kind of message would simply be extra nice to receive.

Consider a personal note a supplement to e-mails and phone calls. When we write one, we're going the extra mile to show we care. When someone receives one, he or she can tell we really put something of ourselves into it—our time, our thought, our effort, our tastes, our personality. And once you learn the six steps, you'll see how quick and easy (and fun!) it can be to write a great note!

the 6 steps to a great **thank-you** note

Remember, thank-you notes consist of six simple parts.

Dear Aunt Dee, ①

Thank you so much for the great new duffel bag. ② ③ _I can't wait
to use it on my spring break cruise_. The bright orange is just
perfect. Not only is it my favorite color (you know that!), but
I'll be able to spot my bag a mile away! Thanks for such a fun,
personal, and really useful gift! _I'm looking forward to seeing_ ④
you when I get back. I'll come over to show you pictures from
the trip! _Thanks again for always thinking of me_. ⑤

Love, ⑥
Maggie

① GREET THE RECIPIENT
② CLEARLY STATE WHY YOU ARE WRITING
③ ELABORATE ON WHY YOU ARE WRITING
④ BUILD THE RELATIONSHIP
⑤ RESTATE WHY YOU ARE WRITING
⑥ GIVE YOUR REGARDS

your turn

You've done plenty of reading so far. Now let's write!

If you're feeling some anxiety about facing that blank sheet of paper, try asking yourself a few of the questions below. The answers will give you some great material for your note.

if someone gave you a gift . . .

- How did you feel when you opened it?
- What words describe the gift itself? The thought behind it?
- What are you doing with the gift now? Be specific.
- If you're not using it yet, do you have future plans for it?
- Why was the gift a particularly good choice for you?
- Does the gift commemorate something? Is it sentimental? Meaningful?
- Does it somehow make your life easier? Better? More fun?
- Did someone have to do something special to make, find, or purchase it?
- If it is a gift of money or a gift card, how do you plan to use it?

if someone provided support or did something kind
for you . . .

- What was it? Why does it deserve special thanks?
- How did you feel when you received the support,
  favor, or help?
- How did the person's timing help make things
  better for you?
- Was the support or help unexpected?
- Has the support or help made your life easier?
  How so?
- Did someone go out of his or her way to help you?
- Did the support or help affect anyone besides
  yourself? Who?
- What qualities must this person have to do what
  he or she did?
- Is there something specific you'd like to do in return?

still stumped?

Need more help? The following pages have lists of just-
the-right words and phrases. And at the end of the chapter,
you'll find lots of sample notes for various occasions.

favorite words & phrases

Using precise, descriptive words can really help communicate your gratitude and make your thank-you note stand out. Here are some of our favorites.

about a gift, event, support, or kindness

Accommodating	*Great*	*Superb*
Beautiful	*Heartwarming*	*Supportive*
Caring	*Helpful*	*Surprising*
Cheerful	*Impressive*	*Sweet*
Compassionate	*Invaluable*	*Thoughtful*
Considerate	*Kind*	*Timely*
Creative	*Loving*	*Touching*
Encouraging	*Luxurious*	*Understanding*
Enjoyable	*Meaningful*	*Unexpected*
Fabulous	*Much-needed*	*Unforgettable*
Fantastic	*Patient*	*Unique*
Fun	*Perfect*	*Useful*
Generous	*Sensational*	*Welcome*
Gracious	*Stylish*	*Wonderful*

about how you feel

Appreciative	*Delighted*	*Honored*
Better	*Eager*	*Hopeful*
Calm	*Enthusiastic*	*Important*
Cared for	*Grateful*	*Impressed*
Comforted	*Happy*	*In awe*

Optimistic	*Relieved*	*Thankful*
Pampered	*Spoiled*	*Thrilled*
Pleased	*Supported*	*Touched*

for gifts

- *How did you know (Sumatra) was my favorite (coffee)?*
- *You have such (impeccable) taste!*
- *What a (snazzy/creative/gorgeous) gift!*
- *I really appreciate it.*
- *It really made my day.*
- *It means so much to me.*
- *It reminds me of (our trip to the beach house).*
- *I have it sitting on my (kitchen table) right now.*
- *Every time I (see it/wear it/use it), I'll think of you.*
- *I'm looking forward to (using/wearing) it for (my trip to Chicago).*
- *It's one of the most (touching/luxurious) gifts I've ever received!*

for support and kindness

- *I can't thank you enough for (house-sitting).*
- *I really appreciate the time you took to (meet me for coffee the other day).*
- *Your help not only meant a lot to me but also (to the kids).*
- *You're a wonderful friend.*
- *Your (advice) has really stuck with me.*
- *Your support helped make this difficult time a lot easier.*

- *(Your story about Jill) really helped put things into perspective for me.*
- *I'm feeling so much better now.*
- *It really helped to not have to worry about (making dinner).*
- *Your fond memories of (Janice) really touched our hearts.*
- *The outpouring of support and love was overwhelming.*
- *(Our mother) would have truly appreciated the (beautiful lilies).*
- *I really appreciate all you did to make me feel so welcome.*
- *Thank you for inviting me and for also including (my friend Phillip).*
- *Thank you for your hospitality.*
- *I particularly enjoyed (the crème brûlée).*
- *I can't remember the last time I (laughed so hard/ had so much fun)!*
- *From start to finish, the (afternoon/evening) was absolutely perfect.*
- *It was so good to (see you/catch up with you)!*

let's review

If you can answer yes to any of the following questions, you know that you've written a great thank-you note.

for gifts

- Can the recipient picture you wearing the scarf she knitted or admiring the flowers she sent?
- Is your note so "you" that the recipient feels like he's actually talked to you after reading it?
- Have you made the recipient feel she's really good at gift giving—especially when it comes to you?

for support/kindness

- Can the recipient tell how much his kindness means to you?
- Does he feel good about himself after reading your note?
- Is the recipient reminded of something special about the evening? Does he laugh about a funny moment all over again?
- Will the hosts gladly invite you back to their home or to their next celebration?

great thank-you notes for gifts

THOUGHTFUL GIFT

Dear Mimi,

Thank you so much for the beautiful guest towels you brought over on Saturday. They are so beautiful, and they match the downstairs bathroom perfectly! It was so nice to have all my friends together in my new place. Hopefully, it's the first of many more gatherings to come! Thanks again for your wonderful gift, and even more—your dear friendship.

Sincerely,
Joyce

THOUGHTFUL GIFT, FOR CHILD

Dear Grandma,

Thank you so much for the handmade doll dresses you sent for Lucy's birthday. I cannot believe you managed to embroider the hems! Lucy loves them so much. When I ask her who they're from, she lights up and says, "Grandma!" We'll treasure them forever. Thanks so much.

Love you,
Alicia

Dear Judy,

Thanks for the homemade pumpkin bread! What a surprise to come in to work on Monday and find such a beautiful (and tasty!) gift. It's so nice to work with someone so thoughtful! Thanks for brightening my day. I'll see you at lunch on Tuesday.

Gratefully,
Connie

GIFT FROM HOME OR GARDEN

Dear Aunt Paula and Uncle Tony,

Thank you for the fifty-dollar check you sent for my high school graduation. What a generous gift! I'm taking a photography class this summer, and I'm planning to put this money toward my supplies. I'm so excited about the class, and this will really help out! It means a lot that you thought of me. I'll be sure to send you some of the photos I take. Thanks again!

Sincerely,
Carlos

GIFT OF MONEY

Dear Mr. and Mrs. Kim,

On behalf of Michael and myself, I want to thank you for the elegant red-wine glasses you gave us for our wedding. They add such a classy touch to our table, and we just love them! In fact, we used them for our first dinner at home as husband and wife! Our wedding was a dream day for us both, and the best part was having our friends and family there to celebrate with us. Thank you for helping make it the happiest day of our lives.

Sincerely,
Laurie Wright-Murray

Dear Aunt Sharon and Uncle Bob,

We absolutely love the beautiful bedding set you gave us as a wedding gift. Thank you! It looks so beautiful and it makes our room feel like a luxury suite! We're really touched by your generosity and all of the effort that must have gone into choosing something that fits our style so well! And having you there to celebrate our special day meant so much to us both. Thanks again for such a wonderful gift.

With love,
Nikki and Matt

Dear Mrs. Rodriguez,

We really appreciate the fruit basket you sent to our family for Christmas. In fact, we had a nice little present-wrapping brunch with all of the contents! We hope that you and Mr. Rodriguez have a wonderful holiday with your family. Thank you for thinking of us in such a thoughtful way.

Happy holidays,
The Georges

GIFT FOR FAMILY

Malcolm,

I just had to sit down and write you a serious thank-you note for the amazing birthday gift from you and the guys. I never thought I'd have a set of golf clubs this nice. Now I really need to work on my game! It was great to have all my buddies together for a day of golfing and goofing off. Now we've got to figure out what to do for your big 4-0! I hope to see you again real soon. Thanks again for everything. What a blast.

Drew

GIFT FROM GROUP

gift from group
It's nice to write a separate note for each person who contributed to a gift for you. However, if the recipients are within close proximity (e.g., if they live or work together), it's OK to send one note addressed to everyone.

for kindness and hospitality

HOUSE-SITTING

Dear Ms. DeGiorno,

Thank you so much for taking such good care of our house while we were out of town this past week. I know that you had to go out of your way to let Pepper out twice a day. I hope you know how much we appreciate your help. You're a wonderful neighbor! We're more than happy to return the favor anytime. Thanks again for everything—and hope to see you soon.

Sincerely,
Kathy Hanson

HELP WITH MOVE

Dear Brian,

Wow—we're moved in! And we simply could not have done it without you. Thanks a million for giving up your week-end to help us. I'm sure you had plenty of better things to do than carry boxes and drive a moving truck around. But we really appreciate it. When it comes time for Lisa's move to the college dorm, you've got a moving crew ready and waiting! Thanks again . . . now on to unpacking!

Sincerely,
Sam and Mariko

Dear Tim,

I really want to thank you for helping me out so much after my knee surgery. From chauffeuring me to my appointments to making sure I had food to eat and clean clothes to wear, you really made my recovery time fly by. It was nice to be able to just focus on healing and getting stronger. Now that I'm on my feet again, I hope I can help you out with your big backyard project. I'll come over this weekend and see how it's going. It's the least I can do to express my thanks.

Talk to you soon!
Mario

HELP WITH RECOVERY

Dear Alan and Linda,

Thank you for hosting such an enjoyable dinner party at your beautiful home on Thursday. What an evening! The meal was outstanding, and Patrick and I are still dreaming of the chocolate cake! We laughed about Alan's joke the whole way home. We truly enjoyed your hospitality, and it was so nice meeting Laura and Phil. We always have such fun with you . . . let's get together soon at our place. Thanks again for a fantastic time.

Sincerely,
Lynn Murphy

DINNER IN HOME

DINNER AT RESTAURANT

Dear Roger,

Thank you very much for dinner at L'Orient this past Saturday. I enjoyed sharing such a delicious meal with you. The food and conversation were exceptional—truly a five-star evening. Thank you, too, for so generously picking up the tab. I'd very much like to treat you to some of Portland's famous seafood when you are here in May. Again, my most sincere thanks.

Regards,
Vanessa Jones

HOSPITALITY

Dear Mrs. Flaherty,

Thank you for inviting me to Thanksgiving dinner. Your house is so cozy and comfortable, I felt right at home. Dinner was great, too. John was right—you are a fantastic cook. Your sausage stuffing was one of the best things I've ever tasted! It was great to spend the holiday with such a fun family. Thanks again for having me.

Sincerely,
Eric Gregorio

Dear Ellen,

I really appreciate all you did to make me feel so welcome this weekend. Your home is beautiful, and you are an amazing hostess. From your fantastic salmon to the relaxing afternoon in the backyard, your warm hospitality just didn't stop! I know how busy you are, and I really appreciate the time it must have taken to prepare for my visit and take such good care of me. I'm looking forward to being able to return the favor someday. Thanks again for such a nice visit.

Gratefully,
Lisa

AN OVERNIGHT STAY

Dear Elissa,

Thank you for the wonderful bridal shower you hosted for me! Everything was perfect—the lilies, the pasta, and especially the punch! Even though you said it was nothing, I know you went to a lot of trouble to pull everything together. I can't wait to return the favor by hosting your baby shower in June! Thanks again for all you did to ensure such a good time for everyone, especially me. You're the best friend a girl could ask for.

Love,
Gayle

HOSTING AN EVENT

A PARTY INVITATION

Dear Stacy,

Thank you for inviting Annie and me to Amy's fifth birthday party. The magic theme was genius—I don't think those little girls have ever had more fun. And the party favors were great! In fact, Annie's still waving her magic wand around the house. I'm so glad that Annie's in school with such great kids, and I'm having fun getting to know all the great moms. Thanks for inviting us!

Sincerely,
Natalie Hartwick

FROM PARTY HOSTS TO GUESTS

Dear Mr. and Mrs. Lansky,

I want to thank you for helping us celebrate my retirement in style. We are so glad you could make it, and we had such a great time with you both. Thank you, too, for the lovely leather luggage tags. I can't wait to book a trip somewhere and travel in style. My retirement party is a night we'll always remember. Thank you for being there to celebrate with us.

With gratitude,
Pam & Richard Jacob

for support and expressions of sympathy

Dear Beth,

Thanks for coffee yesterday. I can't tell you how much our talk helped me put things into perspective. There are few things in life as important as good friends, and I'm really lucky to have one as caring as you. Next time let's get together on a happier note. (And let's go ahead and get the cannolis!) Thanks for being such a good friend.

Love,
Catherine

EMOTIONAL SUPPORT, GENERAL

Hi, Jake,

I want to say thanks for being there for me since I lost my job last month. I really appreciate the time you've taken to listen and to help me see that my job was not the most important thing in the world. Thanks to you, I'm feeling much more optimistic. And no matter what the future holds, I'm keeping our weekly poker game on my calendar! Thanks for being there.

Sincerely,
Nick

EMOTIONAL SUPPORT, LOSS OF JOB

Dear Rob,

Thank you so much for the kind card and all of the support you've given to us this week. Losing our pal Spanky has been difficult, and it's meant a lot that you understand how we're feeling. I really appreciate all of the support you've given us—especially the kids—and for coming over to spend time with us. Looking forward to seeing you soon. Again—thanks so much for everything.

Your friends,
Joanne, Dan, Ethan, and Sophie

Dear Tom,

After a tough couple of months, I wanted to take a minute to thank you from the bottom of my heart for all the love and support you have given me throughout all of this. My father's illness has been heartbreaking for me—and your stories about your dad have really helped me know what to expect and to prepare myself for what's to come. Having you there to listen to me, encourage me, and lift me up when I've needed it the most has made such a difference on so many different days. Thank you so much.

Your friend,
Rose

Dear Maureen,

Thank you so much for all of the support you have given me over the past few weeks. From the numerous tests to the numerous doctor's visits—and all the nervous waiting in between—you've been a real pillar of strength for me through it all. Somehow you knew exactly when to talk, when to listen, and when to let me rant and rave! Even though I'm not sure what the coming months will bring, knowing I have such an incredible source of strength in you makes me feel so much better. Thank you so much for all you've done and continue to do . . . it means the world to me.

Love,
Kevin

EMOTIONAL SUPPORT, ILLNESS

Dear Mr. and Mrs. Jackson,

Thank you very much for the kind sympathy card you sent. It was a really beautiful card, and it was very thoughtful of you to think of our family. Your supportive words and warm wishes mean a lot. Thank you again for your kindness.

Sincerely,
The Greene family

EXPRESSION OF SYMPATHY, GENERAL

Dear Mr. and Mrs. Davidson,

On behalf of my mother, my two sisters, and our families, I want to thank you for the touching card and beautiful flowers you sent following the loss of my father. It meant a lot to us for you to honor his memory in such a thoughtful way. We especially liked the story you shared in your card about one of Dad's famous practical jokes. It really is a comfort to know that you have such good memories of him, too. We truly appreciate your thoughtfulness.

Sincerely,
Claudia Levin

Dear Dr. and Mrs. Patel,

Thank you so much for the kind condolence note you sent after Dottie's passing. Thank you, too, for the generous contribution you made in her name to the Wellness Foundation. I know that Dottie would have been as honored and grateful as I am. Your kind words and warm thoughts helped make a very difficult time a little easier. Thank you again, so much.

Sincerely,
André Dennis

Dear Martin and Marie,

I want to thank you both so much for all of the help and support you have shared with me since Frank's passing. The past month has been a real blur for me, and you were always there to lend a hand, to listen, and take care of so many details for me. Though the months ahead are sure to be a difficult adjustment for me, knowing I have two lifelong friends by my side really makes it all feel more manageable. Thank you so much—for everything.

Sincerely,
Loretta

HELP AFTER A DEATH

Dear Zoë,

Thank you for the wonderful card and flowers you sent this past week. They were an unexpected ray of sunshine in a gray day. It's hard to believe it's been almost six months since Janelle's death. Her birthday was a strange and difficult day for us, and knowing that you were thinking of us was really touching. Thanks for your thoughtfulness and your love—we truly appreciate it.

Sincerely,
Alan and Patricia

FOR SYMPATHY FOLLOW-UP

Notes of
Support & Sympathy

When someone in our lives is upset, sick, grieving the loss of a loved one, or just having a rough time, of course we feel for them. We truly do care. But if we don't communicate those feelings, whether because we're too busy or we're afraid of saying the wrong thing, we can inadvertently send the message that we don't care all that much.

That's where great notes come in. By sitting down and writing a support or sympathy note— no matter how short—we send a little comfort to someone when he or she needs it most. Far from sending the wrong message, we send a message that's very simple, very appreciated, and very right: I care about you.

Sympathy notes always present a special challenge. Most everyone who has ever had to write one has been faced with the same thought: what can I possibly say? Sometimes there's a great deal you can say. Sometimes there is no real answer. But this chapter will help you get through the sympathy note writing process and, hopefully, make that daunting task feel a bit more manageable.

why support & sympathy notes matter

The most comforting sympathy notes and notes of support have one thing in common—they are a unique expression of care and concern. A great support or sympathy note can really help ease a person's pain, and all it takes is a few minutes and a few short lines to remind someone that he or she is in your thoughts during a tough time.

reasons for sending

Life presents us with all sorts of challenges, from minor setbacks to major upheavals. And while the reasons for sending a note of support can vary, the outcome is usually the same. The note's recipient will be comforted by your efforts to show him or her you care. Sometimes—as is the case with sympathy—it may be obvious when to send a note. For other occasions—such as divorce, illness, or just the blues—you may be unsure. Follow your instincts, and when in doubt, send a note. You'll be glad you did.

a few reasons for notes of support

- death of a family member or friend
- minor illness
- a recently diagnosed serious illness
- while fighting a serious illness
- an accident
- before surgery or treatment
- while recovering from surgery or treatment
- chronic health issues
- health concerns for partner or child
- divorce or breakup
- financial trouble
- loss of job
- workplace challenges
- theft, fire, or other material loss

- injury, illness, or death of pet
- new-baby stress
- fertility concerns
- miscarriage or difficult pregnancy
- family challenges

timing

Do your best to send your note of support within a week of hearing the news. But remember—a belated note will also be welcome. And don't feel limited to sending that one, perfect note. Many situations that call for a note of support are ongoing, so you may end up wanting to send notes every couple of weeks—or whenever you think the recipient could use a little pick-me-up.

Send a sympathy note as soon as possible after hearing about a death. If you're late in learning about it, let the recipient know you just heard the sad news. If you're late in sending your note, let her know that she's been in your thoughts. A note might also be welcome after the initial outpouring of sympathy has slowed down.

the power of the sympathy note

Almost everyone struggles with sympathy notes. Sometimes you just don't know what to say. You want to provide some comfort and pay respect to the person who's passed away, but you certainly don't want to make recipients feel any sadder than they already do.

The thing is, no matter how hard sympathy notes are to write, they're some of the most important notes people will ever receive. Reaching out with kind words, shared memories, heartfelt wishes, or offers of help and support will almost certainly help ease the pain of someone going through this most difficult time. When asked what they remember about periods of bereavement, people often cite notes from friends and family—reminders of love and caring that helped bring them through a really diffcult time.

sympathy follow-ups

A sympathy follow-up note offers much-needed (though often overlooked) support during the difficult transitional months following a death. This kind of note simply says you're still thinking about the recipient, you're still there for him or her, and you still want to help, if you can. A sympathy follow-up can include an invitation to get together or an enclosure such as a magazine article; photo; or gift card for a restaurant, movie, or any other thing the recipient enjoys. Consider sending sympathy follow-up notes anytime, but particularly on difficult days, such as the deceased's or survivor's birthday, a wedding anniversary, Christmas or other important holidays, the anniversary of a death, or any other time a grieving person might need a little extra support.

FAQs

I JUST WISH I COULD DO MORE. DO YOU HAVE ANY SUGGESTIONS FOR ADDING SOME EXTRA COMFORT AND CHEER TO A NOTE OF SUPPORT?

This is a common feeling. Unfortunately, sometimes there just isn't all that much one can do to help someone who's going through a hard time. But you can bet that your note will be welcome. It will remind that special person that you are there and you're thinking about him or her.

You might consider adding an inspiring quotation, a humorous or comforting phrase, or a biblical verse to your note. Just be sure it's something he or she would appreciate and is appropriate for the situation. Also take care to quote and attribute it correctly.

For recipients on the mend, emotionally or physically, you could consider sending small gifts—something that will help them enjoy themselves (such as reading materials, music, photos, or treats) or something that will help them relax (like bubble bath, lotion, or pajamas). Consider, too, gift cards to a favorite restaurant, salon, bookstore, or shop. Sometimes a little indulgence is great medicine.

I'M NERVOUS ABOUT SYMPATHY NOTES. WHAT IF I
SAY SOMETHING THAT WILL MAKE THE PERSON FEEL
EVEN WORSE?

Don't be nervous. It's not always easy to find the
"perfect" words. Let your relationship with the recipient
and with the person who's passed away be your guide.
Trust your feelings—and don't be afraid to express them.
The fact is, sometimes there are no perfect words. But
the simple act of reaching out with a personal note is a
perfectly kind and thoughtful thing to do.

Now if you are still worried, you might be reassured
by some helpful words and phrases, as well as some other
words and phrases we recommend you try to avoid.

the 6 steps to a great support or sympathy note

   While the specific situations that call for a support or sympathy note vary, the basic design of such notes is the same. It's the detail and level of warmth that you add that make your notes one of a kind. Ready to get started? Just follow the steps below.

Dear Dave, —①

We're both thinking of you as you recuperate ② *from your hip surgery. It must have been a very difficult couple of weeks.* ③ *Knowing you, you'll probably want to go dancing right away, but we hope you'll take the time to relax and spoil yourself a little as you heal. We're looking forward to visiting you* ④ *this weekend. Until then, take good care, and know we're thinking of you.* ⑤

Sincerely, —⑥
Roger and Gertie

   ① GREET THE RECIPIENT
   ② CLEARLY STATE WHY YOU ARE WRITING
   ③ ELABORATE ON WHY YOU ARE WRITING
   ④ BUILD THE RELATIONSHIP
   ⑤ RESTATE WHY YOU ARE WRITING
   ⑥ GIVE YOUR REGARDS

your turn

With support and sympathy notes, it's often hard to know where to start. If the blank paper is just too scary, have a look at the questions below and think about how you'd reply. Your answers will be the foundation of your note.

if someone needs support or care . . .

- How serious is the situation?
- How did you find out?
- What feelings are associated with the situation—both for the recipient and for you?
- Can you share a story or memory that might cheer up the recipient?
- Been there yourself? What would you have wanted to hear?
- What personal qualities will help the recipient through this difficult time?
- Is she in your thoughts or prayers?
- Are you looking forward to visiting her soon?
- If the person is not going to get better or recover completely, what do you wish for him or her? Comfort? Peace of mind? Presence and support of loved ones?
- Would you like to do something specific to help?

if you'd like to express your sympathy . . .

- How did you hear about the death? How did you feel when you found out?
- What good things do you remember about the deceased?
- What were some of his or her unique qualities?
- Do you have an anecdote, memory, or funny story about the person that you think your recipient would appreciate or enjoy?
- Will you or other people especially miss the person? Why?
- Is there anything in particular that will always remind you of the deceased?
- Are you thinking of or praying for the recipient?
- What can you wish for him or her at this time?
- Would you like to do something specific to help out?
- Have you lost a loved one? What was comforting to you?

need more support?

We've included some words and phrases on the following pages to help you express your support or sympathy. And at the end of the chapter, there's a wide range of sample notes.

favorite words & phrases

It can be hard to find just the right words for notes of support and sympathy. Some sample words and phrases are listed on the following pages, but you'll want to rely on your knowledge of the recipient to choose the words that will comfort him or her. As for sympathy notes, draw on your own memories and feelings about the person who's passed away. Be yourself, and allow yourself to express your sadness. The recipient will appreciate it more than you know.

for support

ABOUT THE SITUATION

Challenging	Disheartening	Overwhelming
Complicated	Distressing	Painful
Confusing	Exhausting	Shocking
Demanding	Frustrating	Tough
Devastating	Hurtful	Trying
Difficult	Intense	Upsetting

ABOUT THE RECIPIENT

Adaptable	Devoted	Positive
Amazing	Feisty	Remarkable
Bighearted	Kind	Resilient
Brave	Loving	Spirited
Courageous	Patient	Strong
Determined	Persistent	Tough

WISHES FOR THE RECIPIENT

Calm	*Healing*	*Rest*
Cheer	*Hope*	*Serenity*
Comfort	*Peace (of mind)*	*Speedy recovery*
Contentment	*Perspective*	*Strength*
Good spirits	*Relaxation*	*Time (to recover*
Happiness	*Relief*	*or adjust)*

for sympathy

ABOUT YOUR FEELINGS

Deep	*Sad*	*Sorry*
Deeply	*Saddened*	*Sympathy*
Grieved	*Shocked*	*True*
Profound	*Sincerely*	*Truly*
Profoundly	*Sorrow*	*Upset*

ABOUT THE DECEASED

Admired	*Honorable*	*Respected*
Caring	*Kind*	*Special*
Considerate	*Loved*	*Sweet*
Dear	*One of a kind*	*Unforgettable*

WISHES FOR THE RECIPIENT

Comfort	*Hope*	*Peace*
Consolation	*Love*	*Solace*
Healing	*Memories*	*Support*

for support

- *I just heard about (your accident), and I'm thinking of you.*
- *I'm deeply sorry to hear (about your sister's diagnosis).*
- *I'm wishing you (comfort) during this difficult time.*
- *My heart goes out to you.*
- *I hope you're (taking it easy).*
- *You've been so (brave); I really admire your (courage).*
- *I'm praying you'll have (strength) when you need it most.*
- *(Our love and support) are always here for you.*
- *We can't wait to see you doing the things you enjoy again!*
- *The weeks ahead will be challenging, and I want to help.*
- *I'm looking forward to visiting you (this weekend).*
- *I'd love to (bring dinner over on Monday night).**
- *Let's (have coffee). I'll call in a few days to set up a time.**

for sympathy

- *I was so sorry to hear that (your father) passed away.*
- *Please accept my heartfelt sympathy on the loss of (your brother).*
- *I'll never forget his story about . . .*

- *I'll always remember the time…*
- *She was such a (kind and loving) person.*
- *She was someone who (always had time to lend a hand).*
- *(Your grandmother) was so proud of you.*
- *Her (generosity) was something I've always admired.*
- *Our love and support are always here for you.*
- *The weeks ahead will be (an adjustment), and I'm here to help.*
- *Jon and I would like to clean the house for you this weekend.**
- *I'll give you a call on Thursday.**

> *Be sure to follow through on any offers or promises you make.

a note on sympathy

As we said, sympathy notes are the toughest kind to write. Your words have tremendous power and can go a long way toward making a difficult time a little easier. Unfortunately, words that aren't quite right may send the wrong message to someone who's grieving. Here is a short list of phrases you may wish to avoid—and why.

- *I know how you feel.* Even if you have experienced a similar loss, you don't want to minimize the recipient's grief.

- *She's in a better place. He's at peace now. It's part of God's plan.* Even if the recipient believes these things to be true, they may be difficult to accept if she's feeling any of the pain, heartbreak, or anger associated with losing a loved one.

- *He lived a long, full life. She was so young.* Focus on what made the person memorable and special, not on his or her age. No matter how old someone is when he or she passes away, it is never easy for loved ones to say goodbye.

- Anything that focuses on the details of an illness, death, accident, or manner of death, or anything that dwells on the negative, such as: *You should never have to bury a child. You never stop needing your mom. What a loss.*

- Try not to give advice or make predictions. Grieving people often feel very alone in their pain, and phrases beginning with *You should* or *You will probably feel* may run the risk of appearing insensitive.

- *Call me if there's anything I can do.* Someone who's grieving is unlikely to take the initiative in asking for help. Instead, do that work for them by making a specific offer of help or support. Depending on how close of a relationship you have with the recipient, consider offering to bring by meals, provide help with housework or yard work, or assist with errands or child care. Even if the recipient doesn't take you up on your offer right away, keep asking. Chances are he or she will need to be reminded you're there.

let's review

If you can answer yes to any of the following questions, you know that you've written a great support or sympathy note.

for support

- Will the recipient really know—and feel—that you're thinking of her?
- Will she chuckle—even though it makes her stitches hurt?
- When she puts your note down, will she be comforted? Will she feel hopeful? Relieved? Reassured?

for sympathy

- Does the recipient know he's in your thoughts or prayers?
- Will he know he's not alone in missing his loved one?
- Might he even smile at a fond memory or funny story?

great support notes

A MOVE

Dear Viv,

I'm thinking about you as you get settled in your new city! I know the move has been really overwhelming—from finding an apartment, to figuring out the subway...not to mention adjusting to the new job! But you know what else? I'm so proud of you! For so long you've been dreaming of working at a magazine and just look at you now! Even though you're not 5 minutes away anymore, I still think of you so much. And I can't wait to visit once you get settled. In the meantime, know I'm cheering you on. And anytime you want a little dose of home, call me!

Love you!
Your Sister

NEW PARENT

Hi there, new mama!

Just wanted to let you know how much I enjoyed talking with you this past weekend. I also want you to know I'm thinking about you as you adjust to life with little Riley. I know what a hormonal, sleep-deprived time this is, but I also know what a tough cookie you are. You're going to have the whole mom thing down in no time. I'm really looking forward to visiting next week. And I'm coming to H-E-L-P, so get ready to relax for a little while. I can't wait to see you both!

Lots of love,
Paige

Hey, Greg,

I just wanted to send a little note to let you know you're on my mind. I know you've been down lately, and I was wondering if there was anything I could do to cheer you up. I'm planning on watching the game at home on Monday night and was hoping you'd join me for a little football and junk food. What do you think? Meanwhile, I'm thinking of you and hoping to see you soon.

Joe

FEELING DOWN

Dear Hal and Sandy,

Lane recently told us about the fire at your lake house—and we were so sorry to hear the news. I know how much you love going up there since you retired, and I hope that you're soon able to get it fixed up better than ever. If there is anything we can do to help out, please know we're here for you. Again, we're so sorry to hear about your loss, and we're thinking of you both.

Sincerely,
Brent and Nicole

MATERIAL LOSS

LOSS OF JOB

Dear Kent,

I read in the Sunday paper that Smith & Smith closed its office here in town, and I couldn't help but think of you. I know the company meant a lot to you. Your talent, work ethic, and worlds of knowledge have been an inspiration to me. I know you'll make the best of this. When it's good for you, let's go grab a bite to eat together. I'll give you a call this week. Until then, you're in my thoughts.

Sincerely,
Jamal Warner

DIVORCE

Dear Deirdre,

I enjoyed talking to you on the phone this past weekend and wanted to let you know how sorry I am to hear that you and Andrew have decided to divorce. I know your relationship means a lot to you, and I know how hard you've been working on it. This must not have been an easy decision. I truly admire the strength you've shown through-out this difficult process. Like you said, the days ahead are going to be a challenge. Please know that anytime you want to talk, I'm here for you. I know you'll get through this.

Sincerely,
Sonja

Hey, Big Guy!

I wanted to wish you a speedy recovery from your foot surgery. It's just not the same around the office without you! I miss your wisecracks more than I ever thought I would. I hope you're resting well and getting around all right. If it's okay, I'd like to stop by with dinner on Thursday after work, but I'll call before I leave to make sure it works for you. Looking forward to seeing you soon!

Sincerely,
Chen

MINOR SURGERY

Dear Chris and Holly,

We were both so saddened to hear about the loss of your pregnancy and wanted to tell you we're thinking about you. We know how much you were looking forward to having another child, and we're wishing you comfort and healing right now. Please know we're both here for you to talk or just be together. We'd love to see you soon. In fact, we'll give you a call this week to see if you'd like to have dinner at our house. Until then, we're sending our thoughts and prayers.

Your friends,
Jim and Beverly

MISCARRIAGE

SERIOUS DIAGNOSIS

Dear Cassie,

*I just heard from Melanie about your diagnosis, and I
wanted to drop a quick note your way. I know it's been
a hard couple of months for you, and your strength and
positive attitude have been just amazing. Please know that
I'll be thinking of you and hoping that your treatments go
as smoothly as possible. I'll give you a call next week to
see what I can do to help you get through this. Until then,
you're on my mind.*

Love you,
Kylie

SERIOUS ILLNESS

Dear Paul,

*We heard from Hazel that you will be starting another
round of treatments next week, and we want to let you know
that you're in our thoughts more than ever. What wonderful
strength and humor you've shown through all of this. We
just know that your positive attitude will continue to sustain
your spirits. We want you to know that we're here for you—
to talk, visit, or give you a hand with things around the
house—anytime. We'll give you a call over the weekend to
see what might be helpful. Meanwhile, we're thinking
of you and sending all our love.*

Truly,
Genevieve and Jim

great sympathy notes

Dear Hector,

*I would like to express my deep and heartfelt sympathy
over the loss of your father. What a good and kindhearted
man he was. I thought the funeral service was a wonderful
tribute to him and to all he has done for our community.
He will be missed by so many. I've been praying for your
comfort and will continue to do so. Again, my deepest
sympathy to you and your family.*

Sincerely,
Walter Miller

LOSS OF PARENT

Dear Mark,

*Please accept our deepest sympathy in the loss of your
beloved wife, Nancy. She was such a sweet, gentle presence
in our neighborhood. We'll miss her beautiful smile. We
are praying that healing will touch your family's hearts right
now. We would love to have your daughters over to visit
anytime. In fact, we'd like to help out any way we can.
For now, our thoughts, prayers, and heartfelt sympathy
are with you and your family.*

Your neighbors,
Pete and Eileen

LOSS OF SPOUSE

LOSS OF CHILD

Dear Mr. and Mrs. Gower,

I am so very sorry about the loss of your daughter. I have many good memories of our years at Smith Lake High. She was a person who touched people's lives everywhere she went. I especially remember a volleyball trip our sophomore year when the bus broke down and Shauna managed to get us all out to do jumping jacks. I've never known anyone quite like her, and I will miss her so much. My heartfelt sympathy goes out to you and your family. You're in my thoughts and prayers.

Sincerely,
Yolanda (Alvarez) Baker

LOSS OF YOUNG CHILD

Dear Kyle and Tara,

I'd like to express my sincere sympathy over the loss of your son. My heart goes out to you both. In his time here, I know Spencer was loved deeply by so many. You and your family are in my thoughts and prayers. I'm very sorry for your loss.

Sincerely,
Mary Heinrich

Dear Ellen,

We were deeply saddened to hear the news of Jeremy's death in combat. We had the pleasure of talking with him last May at your parents' house, and we were so impressed by his kind nature and caring heart. We have the highest respect for the sacrifice he made, but we are so sorry for your heartbreaking loss. Ellen, we're thinking of you. May it be a small comfort to know you're in our prayers.

With great sympathy,
Jim and Eva Myers

LOSS OF CHILD, ACCIDENT

Dear Mr. Gorski,

How very sorry I was to hear about your Aunt Mary's passing. She was always such a sweet lady. I remember how she always had her fingernails painted in Springville's school colors during football season. We'll miss seeing her friendly face in the coffee shop. My thoughts and prayers are with you and your family at this difficult time.

With sympathy,
Bertie Jackson

LOSS OF RELATIVE

LOSS OF PARENT, FROM COLLEAGUE

Dear Jane,

I am truly sorry to hear that your mother passed away. I know from the way you always talked about her that she meant a great deal to you, and I'm so sorry for your loss. Please don't worry about anything here at work. Abby and I can manage your accounts for as long as you need to be away. Just take good care of your family and yourself. My deepest sympathy is with you right now.

Sincerely,
Margaret

LOSS OF PET

Dear Frank, Christine, Annie, and Adam,

We just wanted to let you know how sorry we were to hear that Misty died. She was such a sweet kitty, and we're going to miss her jumping into our laps when we come over to your place. Please know we're thinking of you at this tough time. We're so sorry for the loss of your dear friend.

Your neighbors,
Phyllis, Lucas, and Jonah

great sympathy follow-up notes

Dear Dean and Carla,

We know today is a tough day for you—McKenzie would have been 30. Even after all this time, we know how very much you miss her. We miss her, too. You've both done such an inspiring job of turning your grief into helping others— you're a real inspiration to us all. We just wanted to let you know you're on our minds and in our hearts today.

Your friends,
Rich and Sylvia

SYMPATHY FOLLOW-UP, BIRTHDAY

Dear Ron,

I just wanted to let you know you're in my thoughts, especially as the anniversary of Helen's death approaches. I can only imagine all you're feeling, but I want you to know that I'm here for you every bit as much as I was a year ago. In fact, I was hoping maybe next weekend we could take our bikes out to Green Park for a ride. I'll give you a call this week to discuss it. In the meantime, take good care—I'm thinking of you.

Your friend,
Darlene

SYMPATHY FOLLOW-UP, ANNIVERSARY

Notes of Celebration

There's no denying it—life sure can be tough sometimes. But it can also provide us with plenty to celebrate: birthdays, anniversaries, holidays, weddings, graduations, new babies, you name it! There are all kinds of happy days and all kinds of ways to celebrate them. One way to start is with a cheerful personal note. These kinds of notes are easy—and fun—to write. Now that's something to celebrate.

why celebratory notes matter

A really great celebratory note makes a happy day—or a happy person—even happier. It says that you care about him, admire him, or are celebrating right along with him. It's a way to say "Wow! You're amazing!" It's a way to share in someone's happiness. There's a well-known proverb, "a joy shared is a joy doubled." Well . . . we say why not triple or quadruple it with a fantastic personal note?

reasons for sending

Think about some of the happiest moments in your life. Chances are that a good number of them were marked by some sort of event or occasion. And whether grand or simple, it's these special moments—and the people who celebrated with us—that we'll remember forever. Here are just a few occasions for sending celebratory notes, but let life be your guide. If there's an event, achievement, or occasion (no matter how small), celebrate it!

A FEW REASONS FOR CELEBRATION
- Birthdays
- Anniversaries
- Religious rites of passage (baptism, confirmation, bar or bat mitzvah)

- Graduation
- Engagement, wedding
- Pregnancy, birth, or adoption
- Retirement
- New home
- New pet
- New job
- Promotion
- Work anniversary
- Awards or honors
- Sports achievements
- Meeting a personal goal
- Acceptance to school or program

Also consider sending personal notes on holidays
and other special days. Here are a few to remember:

Mother's Day	Memorial Day
Father's Day	Halloween
Grandparents Day	Thanksgiving
Administrative Professionals Day	Christmas
Cancer Survivors Day	Hanukkah
Nurses Day	Kwanzaa
Veterans Day	Easter
New Year's Day	Passover
Valentine's Day	Rosh Hashanah
Chinese New Year	Diwali
April Fools' Day	Eid

timing

Celebratory notes mark good news or a special day, so getting them there before the party's over (so to speak) is important. Try your best to send your note as soon as you hear the news. If it's for a special occasion, arrange for the note to arrive on the special day itself (or up to three days before).

That said, if you're late finding out, it's perfectly okay to send a note that says so. The recipient will understand and be glad to hear from you. And if you have heard the news and you're just plain late, remember this important fact: a belated note is better than no note—just be sure to acknowledge the delay. People will still be glad to know you thought of them.

The winter holiday season is a nice exception to the timing rule. With the volume of mail being processed, it's okay to send your note anytime during the holiday season—which runs from early December through New Year's Day. To avoid the holiday card frenzy, some people opt to send Thanksgiving or New Year's wishes rather than traditional Christmas cards. The bottom line—when it comes to "when to send" holiday wishes—do what works best and makes the most sense for you.

FAQs

SHOULD I INCLUDE A PERSONAL NOTE WITH GIFTS I GIVE?

Of course! Adding a note is a great way to give a gift
that little extra something. Even if you'll see the recipient on her special day, a personal note makes your gift
especially meaningful. Specific memories, thoughts,
or wishes will make her feel like it really is her day.

WHAT ABOUT GREETING CARDS?

Sending greeting cards is a great way to show people
we care, yet the messages most people write in them
tend to be short and somewhat impersonal. However,
there's no reason you can't apply the note-writing process
to greeting cards. The next time you sit down and are
stumped by how to sign a card, run through the six steps
in this book. Following them—just like you would for a
blank note card—can help give the message you write in
your greeting card a little added personality: yours!

WOW! THAT'S A LOT OF NOTES. HOW MANY NOTES SHOULD I BE WRITING?

Friends, family, coworkers, neighbors, classmates,
teammates, teachers . . .we know a lot of people. That
adds up to a lot of good news to celebrate and special days
to remember. And that can get overwhelming.

But we've got good news—these kinds of notes are always optional. That's right, you're not obligated to send a note for every special day on your calendar. That would be nearly impossible—and not much fun. Instead, when things get hectic and your to do list gets long, just write notes to the people who mean the most to you—or for very special occasions. It's completely up to you. Remember, if you keep the note-writing experience enjoyable for yourself, you'll write better notes. So don't stress!

the 6 steps to a great **celebratory** note

No matter what the occasion, great celebratory notes are made up of the following six parts. All you have to do is add the details!

Dear Desi and John, ①

② *Congratulations*, Mom-and-Dad-to-Be! ③ *Charlotte shared your happy news with us, and we couldn't be more excited.* You're both so loving yet easygoing—you're going to make terrific parents. ④ *We can't wait to see everyone when we're in town for Christmas! Until then, our heartfelt congratulations and warm wishes* ⑤ *for a healthy pregnancy and a happy Baby Williams!*

Sincerely, ⑥
Ryan and Sarah Miller

① GREET THE RECIPIENT
② CLEARLY STATE WHY YOU ARE WRITING
③ ELABORATE ON WHY YOU ARE WRITING
④ BUILD THE RELATIONSHIP
⑤ RESTATE WHY YOU ARE WRITING
⑥ GIVE YOUR REGARDS

your turn

There's something to celebrate! Don't get anxious about finding the "perfect" words. Instead, let your feelings about the recipient and the special event guide you to a great personal note. Here are some questions you can ask yourself to get going.

- Why is this person—and celebrating with her—important to you?
- How did you hear the happy news? What was your reaction?
- What do you think the recipient is feeling right now?
- What do you think she'd like to hear most today?
- What's the significance of this special day?
- Will you see her on the special day? If not, when?
- Do you know how she'll be celebrating or spending the day?
- Did the recipient have to work especially hard to get where she is today?
- What admirable qualities helped her achieve this particular honor?
- How will her special qualities help her in the future?
- Why is this occasion important to you?
- What's your favorite thing about her?
- What do you wish for the next year of her life?

- Is there a story related to this event or occasion?
- Can you offer the recipient any help or guidance going forward?

you're ready!

Now use your answers—along with the helpful words, phrases, and sample notes—to put your heartfelt congratulations into words!

favorite words & phrases

Try using some of these words and phrases to really warm up your congratulations!

your feelings/congratulations

Amazed	*Grateful*	*Overjoyed*
Blessed	*Happy*	*Pleased*
Blown away	*Heartened*	*Proud*
Celebratory	*Heartfelt*	*Psyched*
Delighted	*Hearty*	*Sincere*
Earnest	*Impressed*	*Surprised*
Enthusiastic	*Inspired*	*Thrilled*
Excited	*Jazzed*	*Tickled*
Fortunate	*Lucky*	*Well-deserved*
Genuine	*Moved*	*Wholeheartedly*

the news/event/occasion/achievement

Admirable	Happy	Perfect
Awesome	Huge	Praiseworthy
Best	Important	Prestigious
Big	Impressive	Rare
Blessed	Inspiring	Relaxing
Deserved	Joyful	Romantic
Difficult	Joyous	Safe
Enjoyable	Long awaited	Special
Excellent	Meaningful	Super
Exciting	Memorable	Terrific
Fantastic	Merry	Unforgettable
Festive	Nostalgic	Welcome
Fun	Noteworthy	Well-deserved
Fun-filled	Outstanding	Wild
Great	Peaceful	Wonderful

congratulations

- Congratulations to you on (your recent promotion).
- I'm so happy for you!
- It couldn't have happened to a (nicer) (person/couple).
- Bravo!
- What fantastic news!
- You really earned it.
- I was so excited when I heard!
- What (wonderful) news!

- *I can only imagine how (proud) you must be feeling right now.*
- *You should be proud of (all your hard work).*
- *I'm looking forward to (seeing your new home/ watching your career blossom).*
- *You're such a (natural leader/great student).*
- *You're going to make (an excellent manager/ a wonderful father).*
- *I know you're going to enjoy (parenthood/retirement/ your new puppy).*
- *You're so (bright and hardworking)—you're going to make (a great nurse).*
- *Thinking of you at this (exciting) time!*
- *Enjoy every minute of this (special) time in your life.*
- *If there's anything at all I can help with (as you start your new job), please let me know.*
- *This is just the start of many more great things in store for you!*

special days

- *Your big day is here! Happy Birthday!*
- *It's (Mother's Day), and of course, I'm thinking of you.*
- *You're on my mind on (Grandparents Day).*
- *I'm so happy to be celebrating (your birthday/ this holiday) with you.*
- *I hope your day is filled with (relaxation).*

- *On (Administrative Professionals Day), I'd like to take a moment to tell you . . .*
- *Today is the day to celebrate (my gorgeous sister).*
- *May your day be (unforgettable/one big party)!*
- *I hope you'll find a little time today to (pamper yourself).*
- *Today I'm wishing you (a perfect day for golf)!*
- *Know I'll be celebrating you all day long today!*
- *Again, have a (wonderful/beautiful/memorable) day!*
- *You've always known just how to make a holiday special!*
- *Hope your day is (sweet/happy/merry/fun).*
- *My (Valentine's Day) wish for you? That's easy . . .*
- *(Thanksgiving) is about (gratitude), and I'm so (grateful) for . . .*
- *I'm looking forward to (the Memorial Day barbecue)!*
- *Even though you're far away, I'm thinking of you (during Passover).*

great celebratory notes for life events

PREGNANCY

Dear Tamara,

I just found out from Lisa that you and Paul are expecting. What wonderful news! I'll bet you're both over the moon! And I can't imagine how excited Haley must be to be getting a little brother or sister. I hope you'll let me take you out to lunch to celebrate. I'll call you this coming week to work out the details. And again—congratulations!

Sincerely,
Marie Connelly

BIRTH

Dear Melinda and Max,

Congratulations on the birth of your son Liam. Your sister shared the good news (and darling picture—what a cutie!) with us this past weekend. We're so thrilled for you. Know that your happy little family is in our thoughts! Biggest congratulations and warmest wishes to you all!

Sincerely,
Pauline and George Ferrigno

Dear Bridget and Aaron,

Heartfelt congratulations on the adoption of your new baby girl! We just received the announcement and picture, and we are so excited for you. What a beautiful baby! She is going to be such a blessing—and so blessed to have such wonderful parents. We can't wait to see your new family together at Aaron's mom's house next month! Congratulations, friends! We couldn't be happier for you.

Sincerely,
George and Muriel Stein

ADOPTION

Dear Mason,

Even though you can't read this yet, I want to congratulate you on your baptism. I'm so excited to share this special day with you. Even though you've only been with us for a few months, you've already stolen my heart—and everyone else's, too. I can't wait to watch you grow up! May God bless you and watch over you always, my sweet boy.

I love you!
Grandma Jenny

BAPTISM

BAR MITZVAH, WITH GIFT

Dear Joel,

Congratulations on your bar mitzvah. It's such a happy day for you and for the whole family! We know you've worked very hard to get here, and we're so glad we're able to share this occasion with you. In honor of this important event, we've made a donation to the Foundation in your name. We're very proud of you, and we know you're going to continue to work hard and learn a lot. Mazel tov!

Love,
Aunt Jo and Uncle Jack

GRADUATION

Dear Colin,

Congratulations on your graduation! We were so pleased to see you get your diploma. It hardly seems possible that you could be finished with high school already. With your many talents, I know that you'll succeed in college this fall. We look forward to hearing about the many exciting places life takes you, so please keep in touch. Congratulations and best of luck to you!

Sincerely,
Mr. and Mrs. Jackson

Dear Dawn,

On behalf of Vincent and myself, I want to congratulate you and Kirk on your recent engagement. Your mother shared the news with us this past weekend. How exciting! The two of you are a wonderful couple, and I just know you'll have a very bright future together. Vin and I have been married almost forty years and I wish you the same kind of happiness we've always had.

So happy for you both!
Elaine Richardson

ENGAGEMENT

Dear Jasmine,

I want to offer my heartfelt congratulations on your marriage. I'm so happy that you and Mario have found each other. You are a very special couple. I hope your lives are filled with happiness and love . . . from this day forward! Congratulations!

Sincerely,
Roberta Smith

WEDDING

ANNIVERSARY

Dear Maura and Phil,

Congratulations on your silver anniversary! It's hard to believe we were there on that special day twenty-five years ago. And even harder to believe that Phil's still telling the same jokes! But truly, you two are a real inspiration. Your humor, strength, and amazing love for each other have seen you through three moves, two career changes, and raising four terrific kids! We'll be toasting you high and proud on your special day. Warmest congratulations to you both.

Love always,
Nan and Mel

RETIREMENT

Dear Leo,

Congratulations on your retirement! After all those years, you've sure earned it! Of course, the best part is having more time to spend in the great outdoors—and you're retiring just in time for fishing season! Hopefully, I'll see you at the bass tournament this summer. My warmest congratulations and wishes to you, Leo. I hope it's a dream come true.

Your friend,
Gary

for news & accomplishments

Dear Krista,

I am so excited for you! You're going to love being a home-owner. With your great style, I can't wait to see what you do with your new place—especially the garden! I'm looking forward to coming over once you get settled. In the meantime, I'm here if you need any help moving things over, unpacking boxes, or anything else.

Congratulations!
Laurie

NEW HOME

Dear Barry,

Just a note to congratulate you on the newest little member of your family . . . Rosie the Pug! I'll bet the kids are just going crazy for her. She's one lucky little puppy to grow up in a house so full of fun! I can't wait to come meet her in person next weekend. Congratulations, pet owners!

Your sister and doggy-sitter,
Renee

NEW PET

NEW JOB

Dear Aisha,

What wonderful news! Congratulations to you on your new job! We were so excited for you when you told us. You have such a gift for teaching, and we know you're really going to make a difference at your new school. They're so lucky to have you! Congratulations and best wishes in your new position!

Sincerely,
Richard and Joy

PROMOTION

Dear Evan,

Congratulations on your promotion to Senior Designer! I was so pleased to hear the news this morning. You are famous around here for your creativity and vision, and I know those fine qualities will serve you well in your new position. I couldn't be happier for you or for our company. Great work!

Sincerely,
Theresa Young

Dear Derek,

Just a quick note to say congratulations on getting into Whitman University! Lane just told me the news. And I hear you got an academic scholarship, too. Wow! I know what an honor that is and how hard you must have worked to earn it. I can't wait to talk to you about your plans. Again, congratulations! I'm so happy for you.

Your Cousin,
Sam

COLLEGE ACCEPTANCE

Dear Mr. Andersen,

Please accept my sincere congratulations on receiving this year's community service award. I truly enjoyed attending the ceremony recognizing you and the many different ways you've helped so many people in our area. Your dedication, hard work, and generosity are an inspiration to us all. Once again, congratulations on this well-deserved honor.

Sincerely,
Patrice Harmon

AWARD

SPORTS ACHIEVEMENT

Dear Mr. Grey,

Congratulations on winning the marathon this weekend! As an avid runner and longtime resident, I'm so happy to see a local athlete come in first. And as a dad of two young children, I also wanted to thank you for sponsoring the kids' track program. They are both involved and loving it! You're a real hero to them—and to their parents, too. Congratulations again on your win, and best of luck in Boston!

Sincerely,
Jerry Langer

CHILD'S ACHIEVEMENT, WITH GIFT

Dear Pearl,

I just heard you took second place in the school spelling bee! I know how hard you have studied this year and it sure looks like it's paying off. I'm including a gift certificate to the bookstore so you can treat yourself to something special. I can't wait to come visit you next month so you can teach me a thing or two about spelling. Until then, know how proud I am of you!

L-O-V-E,
Grandma

Dear Maxie,

Just a quick note to say congratulations on getting your article published! Your dad told me the great news. I know that ever since you were a little girl, you've dreamed of being a writer. How wonderful that you've made your dream come true. I'll be watching my mailbox for the June issue. I just can't wait to read it. You're the greatest.

Love,
Aunt Pam

ACHIEVING A GOAL

Dear Court and Jayne,

We just wanted to send a quick note before you left to say congratulations on making your lifelong dream come true. Remember when we'd sit on the deck and dream about living in France? I can't believe you actually made it happen! You both have worked so hard for it, and I know you'll do so well. We can't wait to hear all about your new job and new home— and hopefully plan a visit! We're so proud of you both.

Love,
Pat and Fran

REALIZING A DREAM

for holidays & special days

BIRTHDAY

Dear Penny,

I couldn't let the day go by without wishing you a very happy birthday. You're such a sweet person, and I've really enjoyed getting to know you this past year. If next week's not too crazy around here, let's try to get away from the office long enough to go grab lunch together—my treat! As for today—I hope it's absolutely perfect!

Sincerely,
Heather Macy

MILESTONE BIRTHDAY

Dear Steve,

You made it to 50! Happy birthday! I hope you have the kind of day you can only dream about. You know—sunny, no wind, and you finally make par. Hey, it's your birthday, anything is possible! But seriously, I'm thinking of you on your birthday and wishing you a happy year ahead.

Your much younger brother,
Jim

Dear Helen, Will, and Bette,

Season's Greetings from the Collette house to yours! At this happy time of year, we're thinking of you and just how much you mean to us the whole year through. Here's wishing you peace, joy, and lots of memorable family moments this holiday season. We're looking forward to seeing all of you at the Jensens' party!

Fondly,
Elliot, Christie, and Lily

HOLIDAYS

Dear Diane and Terry,

The halls are decked, the cookies are baked, and now it's time for the fun part—sending warm wishes to great friends like you! We sure do wish you lived closer and could just drop by. We miss your bright smiles and wonderful company and are so looking forward to seeing you in the coming year. The happiest of holidays to you both!

Your friends,
Betty and Jim

HOLIDAYS, ACROSS THE MILES

THANKSGIVING,
TO FAMILY

Dear Shelby,

Thanksgiving is all about gratitude, and I couldn't let it go by without letting you know how grateful I am to have you for a sister. We have so many traditions and memories between us—I think of you a hundred times every holiday. So today, know I'm thinking of you with a thankful heart. And no matter how far away you are, there's always room for you at my table.

Love,
April

"HONORING" DAY

Dear Cate,

It's National Cancer Survivors Day, and of course, I can't help thinking of you. It's a day of celebration, and I'm celebrating the incredible grace and courage you've shown these past four years. You're not just a great friend—you're a real inspiration. I'm so honored to have a friend like you. Cate, as far as I'm concerned, today is your day! I hope you enjoy it.

Love always,
Daria

Dear Lauren,

I wanted to be the first to wish you a happy first Mother's Day. It's been so wonderful to see what an absolutely wonderful mom you are to Amy. She's a very lucky little girl who has a lot to celebrate today! I hope you find some time to relax and spoil yourself a little on your special day. No one deserves it more!

Your friend,
Gina

MOTHER'S DAY

Dear Daddy,

It's Father's Day, and I'm getting ready to enjoy a gigantic banana split. I remember an especially hot Father's Day years ago when we made a giant one with an entire bunch of bananas. We were eating that thing for weeks! You're a major part of some of my favorite memories, Dad. Thinking about you on Father's Day, and looking forward to seeing you soon!

Lots of love,
Olivia

FATHER'S DAY

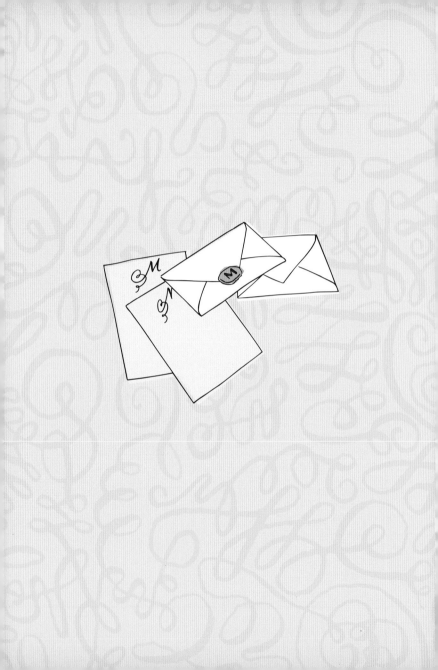

P.S.

But wait, there's more! In the following pages, we've included additional information that goes beyond the paper—and into the envelope and ready to mail! This section covers stationery options, envelope addressing and personalizing, and our Ready-for-Anything Note-Writing Checklist, so you can be sure that no matter what kind of note-necessitating curveball life throws you, you're ready to write.

note-worthy papers

There's a world of stationery out there. Here's a look at some of the most common kinds.

letterhead

8.5 X 11 INCHES

Single sheets that include your name, address, phone numbers, fax, and e-mail. For business, it will also include the company name and your title. Folds in thirds to fit inside envelope. Great for business and profess-ional writing.

letter sheets

7.25 X 10.5 INCHES

Single sheets for more casual notes and letters. Folds in thirds to fit inside envelope. A great choice for longer notes.

correspondence cards

4.25 X 6.25 INCHES

Single panel of heavy card stock. Often monogrammed or imprinted with initials or full name, sometimes bor-dered or embossed. Fits unfolded into envelope but can also be used as a postcard. Very versatile. Good to keep a few on hand.

fold-over notes

SIZES VARY

Folds along top or left side. Front shows illustration, photo, sentiment such as "Thank You," or is blank. Fits closed into envelope. An excellent choice for personal notes—easy to find and thousands to choose from.

paper with personality

Handwritten notes are one of the most personal kinds of correspondence. You can give your note even more personality by choosing a paper that makes a statement—about you or the person you're writing to.

your stationery can reflect . . .

YOUR STYLE AND TASTES

- Have a favorite color or color combination? Play it up.
- Are you a cat lover? Send an animal charity card or paper with paw prints.
- Proud of your Italian heritage? Pick up some art cards or stationery with a beautiful Florentine pattern.

YOUR RELATIONSHIP WITH THE RECIPIENT

- If you're in the same book club, look for cards with quotations or a literary design.

- Writing a thank-you for a night on the town? Try some cool cocktail-themed stationery.
- Is it a note following a particular event? Incorporate a photo into the design.

THE OCCASION AND SEASON

- For birthdays, consider balloons, confetti, bright colors and patterns.
- Have fun with gifts. Try writing your note on an over-sized gift tag.
- Use paper with colors and graphics that reflect the season or holiday.

WHO YOU ARE

- Look for scenes from where you live (landscapes, attractions, or monuments).
- Find papers that represent what you do for a living or as a hobby (stethoscope, music notes, knitting needles, etc).
- Monograms are always a simple and elegant choice. (You can order custom note paper or make your own on the computer.)

THE TONE OF THE NOTE

- For sympathy or difficult situations, a simple paper with minimal design keeps the focus on your important message.

- Go bold with love notes. Think animal prints and hot colors.
- Feeling whimsical? Notes for kids? Rubber stamps, stickers, and doodles are fun embellishments. Or fold your note into a paper airplane.

envelope how-tos

the address

Here's what you need to include on your envelope:

Recipient's Name
Recipient's Address (including house number, street, P.O. box, or apartment number)
Recipient's City and State (Be sure to use the correct two-letter abbreviation)
Recipient's ZIP Code
Country (if not the U.S.)

> Not sure of the state abbreviation, ZIP code, or other information? Find it at usps.com.

Don't forget your return address on the upper left-hand corner of the front or on the back flap of the envelope.

Serious note writers may consider investing in printed labels or an embosser—for a really classy touch.

On an envelope that is hand-delivered, the only thing you'll need to write is the recipient's name.

the name game

The envelope is the first part of your note the recipient sees. While some will argue for the "art" or "rules" of addressing personal correspondence, the fact is, there are many different ways to make sure the recipient gets a great first impression.

How did you address your note? Your envelope should have the same level of formality.

For a note that begins *Dear Dr. and Mrs. Lawrence*, the name line on the envelope should also read *Dr. and Mrs. Lawrence*. First names are optional: follow your instincts on whether it feels right to use them or not.

If your casual note begins *Hey Jack!* you'll probably opt for a simple, casual name line: *Jack Thomas*.

For a note to a couple and their family, there are several different options: *The Montgomery Family; Richard and Georgia Montgomery;* or *Richard, Georgia, Leo, and Trudy Montgomery*. Choose the one that feels right for you and the recipients.

For fun, casual notes, consider using bright, colorful envelopes to really make your note stand out in the mailbox!

Avoid using printed labels if you can, and take the time to make your envelope as personal as your note. There's just something nice about seeing your name in a friend's familiar handwriting.

the ready-for-anything note-writing checklist

If you write notes a lot (or would like to), it might be worth your time to gather some note-writing supplies to keep close at hand. Here's a list of items that will prepare you for whatever note-writing need comes your way.

scratch paper

You might want to jot down ideas and sketch out a note first, just to make sure it says what you want it to before you commit it to fancy note paper.

note paper

Build a collection of notes, papers, and cards (with envelopes!) so you have several to choose from. Consider the events you might write notes for, and make sure you have enough variety to cover those needs.

And when you're out and about, keep an eye out for great stationery. (Craft fairs and clearance bins are great sources for unique, inexpensive papers.)

pens

Consider different color inks and different point sizes for fun and variety.

embellishments

Have a variety of stickers and seals on hand to make your notes—and your envelopes—really unique.

postage stamps

Some notes are planned well in advance, and some are spontaneous, so it's nice to have a range of different postage stamp designs. In addition to any personal or seasonal stamp designs, be sure to have enough basic stamps on hand for serious occasions like sympathy or support.

Remember, postcards and nonstandard envelopes require different postage. It's handy to have a few different stamp values at your disposal.

address lists and cheat sheets

Having an up-to-date address list makes a world of difference for note writing. And a "cheat sheet" will help you remember those important days. Consider keeping a list of birthdays, anniversaries, and special events on your computer desktop so you won't forget to update it.

reference books

You may be amazed at how often you'll consult the thesaurus once you become a regular note writer. Even the experts depend on the old dictionary, thesaurus, book of quotations, or grammar guide from time to time.

parting words

So there you are! Everything you need to write a great note for almost every occasion. And with some practice and plenty of your own creativity, you'll be writing great notes in no time. We have only two more pieces of advice before signing off.

be realistic

Learning how to write a great personal note takes time. You might not write as many notes as you want to right away. That's all right. With our tips and tricks, you'll find writing becomes more natural and more enjoyable as you practice. You'll learn how to write notes more quickly. You'll also learn to tell when enough is enough.

Our advice: take small steps. Promise yourself you'll write one great note this month—maybe a belated thank-you, a great birthday wish, or a heartfelt hello to a friend across the miles. Next month, aim for two. Soon you'll find the notes you have to write become the notes you want to write. And that's really something.

be yourself

It's true—nobody's perfect. Don't feel like you have to use fancy language or perfect grammar. Be yourself—the real, genuine, full-of-personality-and-style-and-even-some-misspellings-here-and-there you. Note writing should be an enjoyable way to reach out and connect, as well as to reflect a little and express how you feel. Being too hard on yourself over details takes a lot of that fun away. So take a deep breath, let go, and enjoy.

about angela

Despite her mother's best attempts to teach her the importance of written correspondence, ANGELA ENSMINGER never had much time to write notes when she was younger. With jobs as varied as Peace Corps volunteer in Morocco and travel writer in New York City, she was always on the go . . . and could never quite figure out the postage.

Then she moved to Kansas City, fell in love, and got married on a beach in Jamaica. Marriage turned out to be a breeze, but writing all those post-wedding thank-you notes was not. There had to be a better way. Something to make it all easier. A system. So Angela studied up on notes and note writing, and soon this book was born.

Now that the thank-yous have all been sent, Angela can focus on her passions—being an editorial director at Hallmark and spending time at home in Riverside, Missouri, with her husband, Aaron, and their herd of cats.

about keely

KEELY CHACE was always a wordsmith, but rarely a note writer. She was too busy reading and enjoying life in rural Kansas. She would rather have written a poem than a thank-you note any day. But things can change ... and they did.

After getting married and having two daughters, Keely learned a thing or two about writing great notes. From "Thanks for the blender!" to "Thanks for babysitting!" Keely cranked out note after note. And enjoyed writing every one.

When not working on a Mother's Day or birthday card, Keely, a senior writer at Hallmark, can be found tackling a do-it-yourself project at home in Kansas City with her husband, Jason, or teaching her daughters the alphabet.

We like receiving personal notes almost as much as we like writing them. If this book was useful to you, or if you have any comments or suggestions for making it even better, please let us know.

MAILING ADDRESS:
Hallmark Cards
Book Feedback
2501 McGee Street, MD 215
Kansas City, MO 64108

E-MAIL ADDRESS:
booknotes@hallmark.com

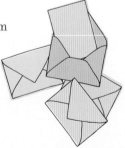